MW01105571

SUICIDE

SUICIDE

BY HAL MARCOVITZ

CRISIS COUNSELING

THERE IS HOPE
MAKE THE CALL

THE CONSEQUENCES OF
JUMPING FROM THIS
BRIDGE ARE FATAL
AND TRAGIC.

Content Consultant
Peter L. Sheras, PhD, ABPP
Curry Programs in Clinical and School Psychology
University of Virginia

ABDO
Publishing Company

CREDITS

Published by ABDO Publishing Company, 8000 West 78th Street, Edina, Minnesota 55439. Copyright © 2010 by Abdo Consulting Group, Inc. International copyrights reserved in all countries. No part of this book may be reproduced in any form without written permission from the publisher. The Essential Library™ is a trademark and logo of ABDO Publishing Company.

Printed in the United States of America,
North Mankato, Minnesota
102009
012010

 PRINTED ON RECYCLED PAPER

Editor: Rebecca Rowell
Copy Editor: Paula Lewis
Interior Design and Production: Becky Daum
Cover Design: Becky Daum

Library of Congress Cataloging-in-Publication Data
Marcovitz, Hal.
 Suicide / Hal Marcovitz.
    p. cm. — (Essential issues)
 Includes bibliographical references.
 ISBN 978-1-60453-958-5
 1. Suicide—Juvenile literature. 2. Suicide—Prevention—Juvenile literature. I. Title.
 HV6545.M255 2010
 362.28—dc22

                                    2009030354

TABLE OF CONTENTS

*On June 28, 2008, model Ruslana Korshunova ended her
seemingly fairy-tale life by jumping to her death.*

DEATH OF THE
RUSSIAN RAPUNZEL

In 2003, Ruslana Korshunova was a
15-year-old girl living in Kazakhstan, a
country in Central Asia. That year, her photograph
appeared in a magazine story about her school's
foreign language club. That picture was spotted by

an executive of one of New York's top modeling agencies. She was struck by the teenager's beauty. "I saw her by chance and she looked like something out of a fairy tale!" said Debbie Jones of the modeling agency Model 1. "We had to find her and we searched high and low until we did! She's really incredible, with feline features and timeless beauty."[1]

Jones's search took her to Kazakhstan, where she whisked Korshunova away. Soon, the teenager was strutting down runways in some of the most important fashion capitals of the world. The young, green-eyed model appeared on the covers of major fashion magazines, earning fees of thousands of dollars an hour. By the age of 20, Korshunova had become one of the brightest young models in the world. The fashion press labeled her the "Russian Rapunzel" because her long and silky chestnut brown hair reached her knees. "She was like an angel," said friend Kira Titeneva.[2]

Feeling Isolated

Ruslana Korshunova may have felt isolated because she lived thousands of miles from her family and spoke little English. Photography studio manager Megan Walsh explained, "A lot of these girls are very young, they're still learning English, and they're expected to be on their own and grow up overnight, basically. They're not ready. I used to be a model scout, and that's why I got out of it. One day, it just hit me . . . 'I can't believe we're taking these young girls from their small towns, be they in Ohio or Estonia. They're not given a chance to be kids and grow up.'"[3]

Although the young beauty had a life many girls dream of, Korshunova was clearly unhappy. On June 28, 2008, her seemingly fairy-tale life ended when Korshunova stepped off the balcony of her apartment in a New York City high-rise. She plummeted nine floors to the street. Many—including friends, family, and mental health experts—wondered why a beautiful, wealthy, and successful young woman would commit suicide. As is often the case with suicides, the question is difficult to answer.

Suicides in Public

Many people witnessed the death of Ruslana Korshunova. Public suicides are common. A study published in the *Journal of Urban Health* examined 7,634 suicides committed in New York City between 1990 and 2004. The research found that 1,853 deaths were from long falls and 334 were from being run over by a train or other moving object—both public acts. The study also found data that suggested people traveled to the city—specifically, Manhattan—to commit suicide.

Such trends have prompted some U.S. city officials to change public facilities to decrease the number of suicide attempts. In 2008, officials in San Francisco, California, approved plans to install a $40–$50 million stainless steel net under the Golden Gate Bridge. The bridge has been the scene of some 1,300 suicidal jumps since opening in 1937.

The New York study found that some people are drawn to tall buildings and bridges that are famous suicide landmarks. Rick Baumann, a suicide prevention counselor in Columbus, Ohio, has noted that people who intend to take their lives in public are seeking attention. They often hope someone will talk them out of killing themselves.

Frequent and Heartbreaking

Suicide is one of the leading causes of death in the United States. Every 16 minutes, a life is lost to suicide. While it is common for young people such as Korshunova to take their own lives, studies show that even younger people commit suicide. The U.S. Centers for Disease Control and Prevention reported that suicide was the cause of death in 4,599 people ages 10–24 in 2004. It was the third leading cause of death for that age group that year. Teenage suicide remains a frequent and heartbreaking cause of death in the United States.

Many people choose death by their own hands. They may suffer from mood disorders, face devastating financial or personal troubles, or abuse drugs and alcohol. Some people who are afflicted with debilitating and painful illnesses may also choose suicide. Kay Redfield Jamison is a professor of psychiatry at

Suicide Definitions

The U.S. Centers for Disease Control and Prevention (CDC) has formally defined suicide as a "fatal self-inflicted destructive act with explicit or inferred intent to die." It also defines "suicidal ideation" and "suicide attempt" as two conditions leading to suicide. According to the CDC, suicidal ideation is defined as "thoughts of harming or killing oneself," while a suicide attempt is a "non-fatal, self-inflicted destructive act with explicit or inferred intent to die."[4]

Johns Hopkins University in Baltimore, Maryland. She stated:

> One would not expect it to be easy to define or classify suicide, and it is not. Death by one's own hand is far too much a final gathering of unknown motives, complex psychologies, and uncertain circumstances. [5]

The effects of suicide can last for years or even decades. Family members and friends suffer from the loss for the rest of their lives. And those who commit suicide often rob society of productive human beings who contribute to the economy and the growth of their communities. Children may have to grow up in families headed by one parent. In addition, the loss of a parent to suicide can devastate children, which may result in alcoholism, drug abuse, and depression. This can put a strain on the social services networks of their communities.

Suicide knows no economic or social barriers. Regardless of one's status in society—rock star, college student, struggling parent, or supermodel— any person can come to the conclusion that death is the only solution to life's problems. These problems may weigh on these individuals in a way that others may never come to know or understand.

Suicide affects more than those who commit the act. Family and friends are left behind, often feeling saddened by the loss of their loved one.

Lonely and Troubled

In the days following the death of Ruslana Korshunova, police and mental health experts tried to piece together the reasons the talented young model took her own life. Clearly, Korshunova had been living a storybook life—she traveled widely, worked in a glamorous industry, and was on the verge of stardom. As police conducted their investigation, a much different picture began to emerge. It was one of a lonely and troubled young woman who seemed overwhelmed by the attention heaped on her and the responsibilities of maintaining a busy and high-profile career.

Korshunova was, after all, plucked out of high school and thrust into the fast-paced world of fashion modeling. At a time when other girls her age may have been studying for their chemistry finals, playing soccer after school, and going to dances on weekends, Korshunova was leading a very grown-up life. She was preparing for model shoots, traveling on transcontinental flights, and seeing her image on the covers of major magazines. "She was very innocent, a complete child," said photographer Boris Brul, who worked with Korshunova early in her career. "She had a child's gaze. There was spark in her eyes."[6]

Korshunova did not leave a suicide note, which may have given police some indication of what had been troubling her. Suicide notes are found for only one in four suicide victims, and investigators usually find these notes to be of limited value. Many suicide notes are incoherent. Typically written moments before the suicide victim's death, the notes cite reasons that only the victim may have understood.

But Korshunova did leave some clues. Shortly after her death, New York's tabloid press printed stories suggesting that Korshunova was despondent over breaking up with her boyfriend. When police reviewed Korshunova's postings on an Internet site, they could see how she felt unloved and isolated in a big city. In the months before her death, she wrote:

> *[I]'m so lost . . . will I ever find myself?*
> *It really hurts when someone stops loving you but you continue to love.*
> *[L]ife is very fragile, and its flow can easily be ruined.*
> *I know what it is . . . I know why my other relationships didn't work out [because] I'm unpredictable.*
> *My dream is to fly. Oh, my rainbow is too high.*[7]

Suicides in New York City

Despite living in a city with a cold and unfriendly reputation, New Yorkers have suicide rates lower than those in the rest of the country, particularly for women. According to the New York State Health Department, the city's suicide rate for women is 2.7 per 100,000 women. The national rate is 4.5 per 100,000 women. Experts suggest the rate may be lower in New York and other big cities because residents have more access to psychiatric help, suicide hotlines, and other suicide prevention services than residents of small towns.

SYMPTOMS OF DEPRESSION

Korshunova's online musings about her failure to find love suggested that she may have been suffering from depression—a mood disorder characterized by feelings of sadness, hopelessness, and inadequacy.

As many as 9 percent of those who suffer from depression take their own lives.

However, many suicides can also be avoided. This is particularly true for people with depression. Prescription drugs can ease symptoms of depression in many patients. Other psychological interventions are also effective. Sometimes, all a depressed person needs is someone to talk over their problems with them. That is why many cities have established suicide hotlines—telephone numbers suicidal people can call to receive immediate counseling from trained professionals.

Clearly, Korshunova's friends saw her as a happy and carefree young woman. They did not realize that a troubled soul was struggling to find love in a world moving too fast for anyone to notice something was terribly wrong.

Suicide Notes

Few suicide notes give many clues about what may have driven the victim to take his or her own life. "Suicide notes . . . often promise more than they deliver," says psychiatrist Kay Redfield Jamison. "It would seem that nothing could be closer to the truth of suicide than notes and letters left behind by those who kill themselves, but this is not the case; our expectations of how we think people should feel and act facing their own deaths are greater than the reality of what they do and why they do it."[8]

Ruslana Korshunova had a successful career as a model when she killed herself. Her death, like many suicides, was a surprise.

Citizens of ancient societies also struggled with the issue of suicide.
Some philosophers found it acceptable, but others did not.

A History of Suicide

uicide has been a part of human culture
at least since the time of the ancient
Romans and Greeks. The fourth-century BCE
Greek philosopher Aristotle frowned on suicide.
He equated the act to cowardice. But Roman orator

Seneca found suicide an acceptable method of dealing with one's troubles. "This is one reason why we cannot complain of life," he said. "It keeps no one against his will."[1]

By the fourth century CE, suicide had been denounced by the Christian Church, which found it sinful. The church considered those who committed suicide martyrs for Satan. In the early fourteenth century, Italian poet Dante wrote *The Divine Comedy*, an epic poem of Christian afterlife. In it, he placed those who commit suicide in the second ring of the Seventh Circle of Hell alongside other sinners. They were doomed to suffer through eternity in the form of gnarled trees and bushes.

Over the centuries, people who committed suicide were denied burials in Christian graveyards. In England, it was believed the spirits of suicide victims would rise from the grave and seek vengeance against those who had driven them to the act. So, people who killed themselves were often buried at crossroads in

"To kill oneself as a means of escape from poverty or disappointed love or bodily or mental anguish is the deed of a coward rather than a brave man. To run away from trouble is a form of cowardice and, while it is true that the suicide braves death, he does it not for some noble object but to escape some ill."[2]

—Aristotle, Greek philosopher, fourth century BCE

the hope of confusing their wandering spirits. In France, loved ones disgraced by suicides in their families often sealed the bodies of the deceased in barrels and tossed them into rivers or seas. Some suicide victims were hanged from the gallows—after their deaths. In some European cities, the bodies of suicide victims were automatically donated to medical schools for dissection by student doctors.

Antony and Cleopatra

Two of the most famous deaths by suicide were those of Roman General Marc Antony and Egyptian Queen Cleopatra. Following the assassination of Julius Caesar in 44 BCE, Antony married Cleopatra and forged an alliance to challenge Octavian, the future emperor of Rome. Antony's troops deserted him and sided with Octavian. Antony sent a message to his rival pleading for mercy. When Octavian refused, Antony committed suicide by falling on his sword. Octavian made it clear he would return to Rome with Cleopatra as his captive. According to legend, when Cleopatra heard this news, she committed suicide by pressing an asp, a venomous snake, to her breast.

ROMEO AND JULIET

During the Renaissance of the fourteenth, fifteenth, and sixteenth centuries, many scholars wrote books and essays about suicide. They speculated on its causes and motivations. These writings sparked a much more sympathetic viewpoint regarding suicide victims. In the late sixteenth century and early seventeenth century, English playwright William Shakespeare wrote many dramatic plays. Fourteen of his characters committed suicide.

Authors such as William Shakespeare addressed suicide in their writing.

While audiences in London's Globe Theater had no love for Lady Macbeth, they could understand her motivation for killing herself. She suffered from overwhelming guilt after urging her husband to commit murder. But audiences found themselves sharing the pain of Romeo and Juliet. When the young lovers took their own lives, the audience in the Globe wept.

Other writers and intellectuals also wrote sympathetically about suicide, suggesting that people who took their own lives should be regarded more as victims than as sinners. In 1648, the lengthy essay *Biathanatos* by English poet John Donne was published. It declared suicide was not a sin. A similar defense of suicide was advanced a century later in the essay *Of Suicide* by Scottish philosopher and historian David Hume.

Such defenses of suicide helped convince government and church leaders to modify their hard-line positions. In 1823, the British parliament outlawed crossroads burial and ordered that suicide victims be interred in cemeteries. Throughout Europe, church leaders continued to publicly condemn suicide as sinful, but Christian clergymen were permitted to conduct graveside services for victims.

"Mine Own Sword"

English poet John Donne helped change minds about suicide. He argued that taking one's own life was not a sin. Donne said, "Methinks I have the keys of my prison in mine own hand, and no remedy presents itself so soone [sic] to my heart, as mine own sword."[3]

Karl Marx was a nineteenth-century German writer who wrote extensively on suicide, particularly among women. Marx believed the abuse of women and their treatment as second-class citizens was primarily responsible for their suicides. His two daughters, Laura and Eleanor, committed suicide.

SUICIDE IN OTHER CULTURES

Non-European cultures also wrestled with the notion of suicide. In feudal Japan (1200s–1600s), the act of suicide, known as hara-kiri, was accepted as an honorable exit from dishonorable circumstances.

Jonestown Suicides

Perhaps one of the saddest chapters in the history of suicide occurred in 1978. More than 900 members of a cult known as the People's Temple took their own lives in a jungle camp in Guyana, South America. Formed in 1955, the cult centered on an eccentric California minister, the Reverend Jim Jones. He led his followers to the jungle with the promise that they would establish a utopian society away from government control and apart from urban ills such as drugs, crime, and racism. They called their community Jonestown.

Jonestown was established in 1977. In November 1978, reports surfaced that some People's Temple members were being held in Jonestown against their will. Leo J. Ryan, a California congressman, led a fact-finding mission to Jonestown to determine the truth. When Ryan learned that some members did want to leave, he and the members of his group were murdered by gunmen dispatched by Jones. After the attack, Jones ordered a mass suicide. Most of the 918 People's Temple members killed themselves by consuming fruit drinks laced with cyanide; some who resisted were shot. Some members escaped by hiding in the jungle. Jones died of a self-inflicted gunshot wound to the head.

A nobleman known as a samurai was expected to commit suicide for such transgressions as losing in battle or failing to respond to an insult. The preferred method was cutting into one's abdomen with a small sword carried expressly for that purpose—the Japanese words *hara kiri* translate to "stomach cutting" in English.

In ancient India, suicide was regarded as an acceptable alternative to dying from disease. Sometimes, the elderly and the ill starved themselves to death or buried themselves in snow. Others set themselves on fire or threw themselves into the Ganges River to be mauled and eaten by crocodiles.

In the Muslim world, the revered Prophet Muhammad condemned suicide as unholy. But today, some Islamic fundamentalists willingly become suicide bombers. They know they will be killed while killing others. They do not regard the act as suicide but as martyrdom in defense of Islam for which they will be rewarded in heaven.

Throughout history, Jewish scholars have also condemned suicide. But heroes of Judaism include the Zealots. Members of a first-century sect, Zealots took their own lives rather than submit to defeat by the Romans.

THE WISH TO DIE

By the early twentieth century, psychiatry had developed as a science. Physicians began to attribute suicidal ideations to mental disorders. Austrian physician Sigmund Freud's ideas would form the basis of modern psychiatry. In his 1917 essay *Mourning and Melancholia*, Freud suggested that people used suicide as an outlet for their hostilities. He further theorized that people were motivated by the will to live—Eros—and the will to die—Thanatos. Freud believed most people struggled between the two, and when the struggle was won by Thanatos, the result was often suicide.

The American psychoanalyst Karl Menninger expanded on Freud's theories in his 1938 book *Man Against Himself*. Menninger cataloged a number of self-destructive behaviors and declared that three elements must be present in each case of suicide: the wish to kill, the wish to be killed, and the wish to die.

The Suicide of Sigmund Freud

Psychoanalyst Sigmund Freud, whose work helped define the mental disorders that sometimes drive people to suicide, took his own life in 1939. Freud had suffered for years from cancer. He asked his personal physician, Max Schur, to administer a fatal dose of morphine. Freud's last words were, "My dear Schur, you certainly remember our first talk. You promised me then not to forsake me when my time comes. Now it is nothing but torture and makes no sense any more."[4] Schur agreed and injected Freud with a lethal dose of morphine.

Major work in understanding suicide was performed by American psychologist Edwin S. Shneidman. In 1958, Shneidman cofounded the Los Angeles Suicide Prevention Center to better understand suicide and help those who feel suicidal. He concluded that all suicide victims bear intense psychological pain, believe they are isolated from others, and develop the perception that death is the only solution. He said of suicide:

> [It] is unlikely that any one theory will ever explain phenomena as varied and as complicated as human self-destructive behaviors. In general, it is probably accurate to say that suicide always involves an individual's tortured and tunneled logic in a state of inner-felt, intolerable emotion.[5]

Sigmund Freud addressed suicide in his work. He later died by suicide.

Suicide affects people from all backgrounds. However, men commit most of the suicides in the United States.

RISK FACTORS

uicide affects people worldwide. According to the World Health Organization (WHO), suicide has increased by 60 percent worldwide in the last half-century. WHO reported that approximately 1 million people died from suicide in 2000 and that young people have the highest risk of suicide in one-third of countries worldwide.

In its 2008 report on suicide, WHO reported suicide rates for 101 countries. The countries with the ten highest rates of suicide were predominantly Eastern European. They were Lithuania, Belarus, Russia, Sri Lanka, Hungary, Slovenia, Kazakhstan, Latvia, Japan, and Ukraine.

The United States is ranked forty-second on WHO's 2008 suicide report. Suicide is the eleventh leading cause of death in the United States. It accounts for 1.4 percent of all deaths. In the United States, more than 32,000 suicides occur each year—approximately 89 per day. In some age groups, suicide is among the top ten causes of death. In young adults between the ages of 25 and 34, suicide is the second leading cause of death. It is the third leading cause of death in teenagers. Overall, 11 out of every 100,000 U.S. citizens take their own lives.

Leading Cause of Death

According to the U.S. Centers for Disease Control and Prevention, suicide was among the top five causes of death in the following age groups:
- Ages 10–14: fourth leading cause of death
- Ages 15–24: third leading cause of death
- Ages 25–34: second leading cause of death
- Ages 35–44: fourth leading cause of death
- Ages 45–54: fifth leading cause of death

Suicide Rates per 100,000 as of 2008[1]
Most Recent Year Available

Rank	Country	Year	Deaths
1	Lithuania	2005	81.0
2	Belarus	2003	73.6
3	Russian Federation	2005	67.9
4	Sri Lanka	1991	61.4
5	Hungary	2005	53.5
6	Slovenia	2006	53.2
7	Kazakhstan	2005	53.1
8	Latvia	2005	51.6
9	Japan	2006	48.0
10	Ukraine	2005	47.9
11	Guyana	2005	45.4
12	Republic of Korea	2006	43.7
13	Estonia	2005	42.8
14	Belgium	1997	42.6
15	Finland	2006	40.7
16	Croatia	2005	40.2
17	Serbia	2006	39.5
18	Republic of Moldova	2006	36.6
19	France	2005	35.6
20	Switzerland	2005	35.2

Source: World Health Organization

Suicide affects people worldwide.

The number of attempted suicides in the United States is staggering—some 800,000 people attempt but fail to take their own lives each year. For every successful suicide attempt, 25 attempts fail. Former

U.S. Surgeon General David Satcher
stated:

> Suicide has stolen the lives and
> contributed to the disability and suffering
> of hundreds of thousands of Americans
> each year. There are few who escape
> being touched by the tragedy of suicide in
> their lifetimes.[2]

MEN VERSUS WOMEN

The desire to commit suicide can
afflict all types of people, but trends
indicate that some people are more
at risk than others. White males have
the highest suicide rate: nearly 13 per
100,000 people, and men commit
nearly 80 percent of all suicides in
the United States. The suicide rate
for men is four times that of women.
Women suffer from higher rates of
depression than men and make twice
as many suicide attempts. But the
higher suicide rate for men indicates
that they are far less likely to seek help

Men Use Guns

Men are more impulsive
than women when it
comes to suicide—even
in how they do it. According to the U.S. Substance
Abuse and Mental Health
Services Administration,
57 percent of male suicide victims use guns,
compared to 32 percent
of women. Women are
more likely to take overdoses of pills—38 percent
of women and 13 percent
of men use this suicide
method. In addition, 23
percent of men and 20
percent of women use
suffocation to commit
suicide. Because guns
are more lethal than
other methods, men succeed more often, which
contributes to the higher
suicide rate among them.

for their depressive symptoms than women. Men also use methods of committing suicide that are more likely to be fatal.

While men commit suicide more frequently than women, women are twice as likely as men to suffer from depression. Mental health experts believe women tend to be less impulsive than men and so give more thought to the act. Women worry more about how their suicides may affect their family members and friends. They also are more inclined than men to talk about their problems with their friends and doctors.

George E. Murphy is a former professor of psychiatry at Washington University School of Medicine in St. Louis, Missouri. He explained:

> Women process their experiences with friends. They discuss their feelings, seek feedback and take advice. They are much more likely to tell a physician how they feel and cooperate in the prescribed treatment. As a result, women get better treatment for their depression.[3]

Women Worry

Women fret more than men over how their suicides will affect the loved ones they leave behind. Dr. George E. Murphy explained, "She'll consider not just her feelings but also the feelings of others—her family, the children, even acquaintances, and how those people will be affected by a decision like suicide. A man is much less likely to take those things into account. He makes his decision, and it's about him, so he doesn't feel the need to share it with anyone else."[4]

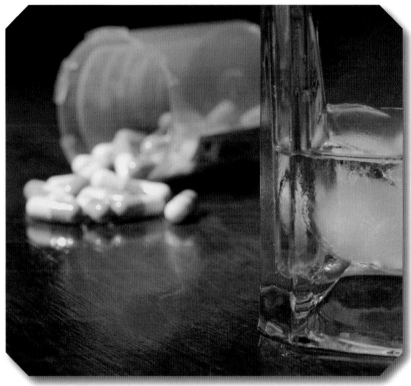

Drugs and alcohol often play a role in suicide attempts.

ALCOHOL AND DRUGS

Certainly, mood disorders are the root cause of most suicide attempts. According to the National Institute of Mental Health, 90 percent of all people who commit suicide are suffering from some degree of illness—usually depression—at the time of their deaths.

Often, though, other factors combine with mental disorders to enhance the risk of suicide. For example, people who commit suicide are also likely to abuse drugs and alcohol. A 2005 study of suicide in 13 states found that as many as 70 percent of suicide victims had high concentrations of alcohol in their blood at the time of their deaths. Many people drink heavily shortly before they make the decision to take their own lives. The authors of the study suggested that alcohol promotes impulsive behavior, which helps the drinker make the final decision to commit suicide. The authors found that heavy drinking enhances the probability of a suicidal act by a staggering 90 times.

Moreover, the study also found that heavy drinking prompts suicidal people to search for the most lethal means of killing themselves—usually guns. This means that heavy drinkers often succeed when they finally resolve to take their own lives.

Drug abuse also enhances the likelihood of suicide. In 2008, the U.S. Substance Abuse and Mental Health Services Administration studied suicide. The research showed that 19 percent of people treated in emergency rooms following suicide attempts had abused drugs shortly before they tried to take their lives. People who suffer from depression often abuse drugs to escape their troubles. Similar to alcohol, drugs often promote impulsive behavior.

THOSE MOST AT RISK

Suicide rates vary by race and ethnicity. Some groups suffer from higher rates of suicide than others, often as a result of social factors that can affect every facet of a person's life. Some groups face greater social and economic challenges, which can result in higher rates of poverty, depression, and substance abuse. In 2008, the Centers for Disease Control

Military Suicides

The stress felt by soldiers on the battlefields in Afghanistan and Iraq has led to an increase in the number of suicides among members of the U.S. military. In 2008, 128 members of the U.S. Army took their lives—the highest level since the United States invaded Afghanistan in 2001 and Iraq in 2003.

In 2008, the suicide rate for the U.S. Army was 20.2 per 100,000 soldiers. This was approximately twice the overall U.S. civilian rate of 11 per 100,000 people. Moreover, the U.S. Army reported that 24 soldiers took their own lives in January 2009. "There is no doubt in my mind that stress is a factor in the trend we're seeing," said General Peter Chiarelli, U.S. Army vice chief of staff.[5]

In 2008, nearly one-third of army suicides occurred among soldiers deployed in Iraq and Afghanistan. Another third occurred among soldiers who had not yet been deployed to the war zones. The remainder occurred among soldiers who had recently returned home. A large majority of suicides—78 percent—were committed by soldiers serving their first tour of duty.

and Prevention (CDC) reported that suicide is the second leading cause of death among young American Indians/Alaska Natives ages 15–34. The suicide rate for this group is almost 22 per 100,000 people. That is twice the U.S. average of 11 suicides per 100,000 people.

The CDC also noted in 2008 that Hispanic female high school students attempted suicide more often than other female high school students. Fourteen percent of Hispanic young women in grades 9–12 reported suicide attempts, compared to 9.9 percent of black, non-Hispanic female high school students and 7.7 percent of white, non-Hispanic female high school students.

ECONOMIC CLIMATE

Factors other than sex, substance use, and ethnicity contribute to suicide. Debilitating physical illnesses can lead people into states

The Highest Suicide Rates

The highest suicide rate for any group is men over the age of 85. According to the National Center for Health Statistics, almost 17 percent of men in that group commit suicide every year. The second-highest suicide rate includes men between the ages of 75 and 84. Approximately 16 percent of men in this age group take their lives each year. The U.S. Substance Abuse and Mental Health Services Administration found that men in these two age groups are most likely to be widowed or divorced and suffering from debilitating illnesses.

of depression and, ultimately, suicide. That is why people over the age of 65 are among those most at risk for suicide—they suffer illnesses far more often than younger people. According to statistics compiled in 2005 by the CDC, approximately 15 of 100,000 people over the age of 65 commit suicide.

However, trends indicate that more people between the ages of 40 and 64 are emerging as a group at risk for committing suicide. From 1999 to 2005, the rate of suicide in that age group went up 2.7 percent annually for men and 3.9 percent annually for women. Researchers also believe the economic woes that surfaced in 2007 and 2008 in the United States and other countries have increased the occurrence of depression and are contributing to the continuing rise in the suicide rate among middle-age adults. Psychologist Seetal Dodd, a senior fellow at the University of Melbourne in Australia, explained:

> There is a considerable risk that the current economic situation may result in a further spike in the suicide rate for men of working age, especially if we start to see an increase in unemployment and a decrease in housing affordability and consumer sentiment.[6]

"[W]hether the act of an impulsive teenager, a depressed business-man, or a terminally ill cancer patient, a suicide leaves behind a great many victims—wife, hus-band, parents, children, friends—for whom the pain is just beginning."[7]

—*George Howe Colt,*
The Enigma of Suicide

Indeed, when people lose their jobs, their homes, and their bank accounts, it may seem to them as though the world is falling apart. They may seek escape from their woes in alcohol or drugs. They may also turn to much more drastic resolutions to their problems, including ideas about and attempts at suicide.

A failing economy can result in job loss and financial worries
that lead to an increase in depression.

Depression causes many people to feel sad, worthless, and hopeless.

MENTAL DISORDERS AND SUICIDE

evere depression can often lead to suicidal ideations. The disorder interferes with the ability to work, study, sleep, and otherwise enjoy life. People who are depressed are consistently sad, pessimistic, and anxious. They may feel their

problems are too overwhelming to overcome, and
they may have feelings of guilt. They experience a
decrease in energy, an inability to concentrate, and
often a change in their eating habits. They may feel
chronic physical pain. Finally, if their depression
is untreated, sufferers may begin to think about
suicide, and these ideations may begin to dominate
their thoughts. As many as 8 percent
of people with depression take their
own lives.

Depression is regarded as an
affective, or mood, disorder.
Everyone has moods—we may feel
happy, sad, optimistic, pessimistic,
fearful, or calm. Usually, moods
change because of external factors—if
someone feels sad and receives good
news, chances are his or her mood
will brighten. In depressed people,
moods change because of their
mental disorder rather than as a
result of external factors.

Approximately 12 million people
in the United States suffer from
depression. Kay Redfield Jamison

Depression: A Firsthand Account

Book publisher Paul Gott-
lieb endured depression
for many years and often
had suicidal thoughts. He
said, "You are pushed to
the point of considering
suicide, because living
becomes very painful.
You are looking for a way
out . . . to eliminate this
terrible psychic pain. . . . I
never really tried to commit suicide, but I came
awful close, . . . I would
walk out into traffic of
New York City, with no
reference to traffic lights
. . . almost hoping that
I would get knocked
down."[1] Gottlieb died
from a heart attack
in 2002.

of Johns Hopkins University says of depression and suicide:

> [S]ome type of depression is almost [constant] in those who kill themselves. An estimated 30 to 70 percent of people who kill themselves are victims of mood disorders; the rate is even higher when depression co-exists with alcohol or drug abuse.[2]

Repeat Attempts

A 2008 study by Swedish university Karolinska Institutet investigated repeat suicide attempts among 40,000 mentally ill patients. The study found that bipolar and schizophrenia sufferers who attempt suicide are likely to make a second attempt within a year of their first try. It found that more than half of those who made second attempts within a year of their first were successful.

Bipolar Disorder

Depression is not the only illness that can lead to suicide. A mood disorder known as bipolar disorder has also been found at the root of many suicides. Approximately 5.7 million people in the United States are believed to suffer from bipolar disorder.

Also known as manic depressive illness, the disorder includes elements of depression. Bipolar sufferers often sink into severe periods of depression, then enter manic phases that feature episodes of extreme euphoria and hyperactivity.

These mood swings are often quick and extreme. People with bipolar disorder are much more impulsive than people who are depressed—a factor that may lead to suicide. Also, those who are bipolar are considered more difficult to treat. During their manic phases, they feel good and often stop taking their medications. Soon, though, the euphoria ends and becomes an episode of depression that may lead to suicidal ideations. These factors contribute to the high suicide rates among bipolar patients—as many as 15 percent take their own lives.

Untreated bipolar disorder is believed to have been responsible for the suicide of Kurt Cobain, one of the top rock stars of the 1990s. Cobain was leader of the band Nirvana. In January 1992, the band's album *Nevermind* hit the top of the charts. However, Cobain's musical success hid his personal struggles.

Cobain was a deeply troubled individual. In addition to probably suffering from bipolar disorder, he abused alcohol and used heroin. He had a family history of mental disorders and suicide. His marriage to rocker Courtney Love was turbulent. On April 5, 1994, at the height of his popularity, Cobain took his own life with a gun. He was 27 years

Kurt Cobain had a successful musical career when he killed himself in 1994.

old. His cousin, psychiatric nurse Beverly Cobain, stated:

> *Kurt was, without doubt, bipolar—he had a psychological disorder which caused him to swing from wild ecstasy to manic despair. In trying to self-medicate with heroin, he almost certainly made the problem worse. That was the background to his shooting himself.*[3]

Personality Disorders

Borderline personality disorder is another mental disorder that can lead to suicidal behavior. People who are borderline do not suffer from a mood disorder. Rather, their disease is classified as a personality disorder. It prompts patients to exhibit behavior that is outside what is considered normal for their culture. Sufferers have difficulty managing their emotions. The illness is most common among teenage girls and young women. They maintain unstable relationships with other people, often have a poor self-image, and, similar to those with bipolar disorder, are subject to wild mood swings.

People with borderline disorder are impulsive, unpredictable, and self-destructive. They often turn to suicide attempts or self-mutilation to call attention to themselves. John Gunderson, director of personality disorders treatment at McLean Hospital in Belmont, Massachusetts, said:

> The most characteristic feature of the condition is multiple suicide attempts. These attempts usually occur in the context of a problem in a relationship. These patients come into the emergency room, for example, after a fight with somebody, which leads them to take an overdose or slash their wrists.[4]

As many as 2 percent of U.S. teenagers and adults may suffer from some degree of borderline personality disorder. The disorder also has a high rate of suicide—10 to 15 percent of sufferers take their own lives.

Borderline Personality Disorder

Mental health professionals estimate that some 75 percent of patients with borderline personality disorder are women and that, in most cases, the disorder starts manifesting during adolescence. Typically, the first self-destructive behavior exhibited by people with the disorder is cutting themselves, usually with razor blades or kitchen knives.

Those with borderline disorder injure themselves because it is the only way they know to manage their emotions. "I would do it when things got me upset," a 17-year-old borderline patient named Brittany told *Time* magazine. "At the time, it was a relief, until you wake up the next morning, look at your arms and think . . . what did I do?"[5] Many borderline sufferers move on to more self-destructive behavior, including suicide.

Psychotherapist Adolph Stern pioneered the study of borderline personality disorder in 1938. He gave the disorder its name, finding that a particular group of his patients did not respond to psychoanalysis. He described them as existing on the borderline between psychosis and neurosis. Psychosis is a severe symptom of mental disorder in which patients fall out of contact with reality. Neurosis is a milder mental disorder in which patients experience stress but are still able to function with rational behavior.

SCHIZOPHRENIA

Schizophrenia is another illness that can lead to suicidal behavior. This disease is characterized by an abnormal perception of reality. People with schizophrenia are prone to angry outbursts, social isolation, delusional beliefs, and hallucinations. Many times, schizophrenia is worsened by symptoms of paranoia. Patients feel threatened by others. Their overwhelming fear and suspicion can lead them to self-destructive acts.

Approximately 1 to 2 percent of the adult population in the United States is believed to suffer from some degree of schizophrenia. Approximately 10 percent of schizophrenics take their lives.

Schizophrenia plagued Ernest Hemingway, who was perhaps the most influential writer of the twentieth century. He wrote such books as *The Sun Also Rises*, *For Whom the Bell Tolls*, and *The Old Man and the Sea*, for which he won the Nobel and Pulitzer prizes. As he neared the end of his life, Hemingway frightened his friends with his paranoid delusions. The famous author believed the government was plotting against him and that he was constantly followed by federal agents who wiretapped his telephones. Hemingway

Famous Sufferers of Mental Disorders

German composer Ludwig van Beethoven wrote some of history's most familiar music. He is believed to have suffered from depression. He wrote often about death and once attempted suicide. Another German composer of note, Robert Schumann, attempted suicide several times. He had bipolar disorder.

Artist Vincent van Gogh suffered from both bipolar and borderline disorders—he famously cut off his ear. He committed suicide in 1890. Another bipolar sufferer, English author Virginia Woolf, took her own life in 1941. Actress Marilyn Monroe had bipolar disorder and committed suicide in 1962 by using sleeping pills. Mike Wallace of *60 Minutes* suffers from depression.

believed his friends were telling lies about him. He was no longer able to write. He accused his friends, family members, and business associates of stealing money from him. Hemingway's friend, writer A. E. Hotchner, recalled:

> *Basically, Ernest's ability to work had deteriorated to a point where he spent hours with [a] manuscript . . . but he was unable to really work on it. . . . His talk about destroying himself had become more frequent, and he would sometimes stand at the gun rack, holding one of the guns, staring out the window at the distant mountains.*[6]

Hemingway was hospitalized in a psychiatric institution, but his treatments failed. On July 2, 1961, he committed suicide. He was 61 years old.

The Hemingway Family History

People who are bipolar often have a family history of mental disorders. According to the National Institute of Mental Health, 33 percent of bipolar patients have a parent who is bipolar. In the case of Ernest Hemingway, granddaughter Margaux Hemingway was also diagnosed with the disease. Like her grandfather, Margaux committed suicide.

Ernest Hemingway in 1950. The acclaimed author and sometimes larger-than-life personality could not overcome his urges to kill himself.

The challenges young people face can be stressful. Many teens suffer from depression and experience suicidal thoughts.

THE YOUNGEST VICTIMS

oung people may feel stressed, troubled, or depressed for many reasons. They may not be doing well in school. Their parents may be getting a divorce. There may be violence at home. They may have been rejected by friends. Close friends or family members may have recently died. They may be abusing drugs or alcohol. Many motives could prompt a teenager to commit suicide.

According to the U.S. Centers for Disease Control and Prevention (CDC), approximately 4,000 young people under the age of 24 take their own lives each year. Moreover, despite the establishment of community- and school-based intervention programs, suicides by teenagers and young adults are on the rise. From 2003 to 2004, the suicide rate among young people rose 8 percent. "The real importance of this is that it shows a real, fundamental change in the phenomenon of suicide in this country," says CDC physician Mark Rosenberg. "Whereas a few years ago it might have been your grandfather . . . now it's your son."[1]

Suicides account for 1.3 percent of all deaths in the United States. Among teenagers and young adults, suicide is considered the cause in 12.3 percent of deaths. According to the American Association of Suicidology, a young person under

Planning

Suicide among adults is usually regarded as an impulsive act. While that is true for many suicides by teenagers, some young people are also believed to spend months thinking about their own deaths. Psychologist Susan Bartell of Port Washington, New York, says, "Suicide is never something that's literally out of the blue, where you go from being completely fine to trying to kill yourself. Most teens think about suicide a lot before they try it."[2]

the age of 25 takes his or her life every 2 hours and 11 minutes. This adds up to a dozen young people who kill themselves every day.

LEARNING TO DEAL WITH FAILURE

Teenagers face the same mental health issues as adults. Bipolar symptoms often surface during adolescence, while most borderline patients are teenage girls. These conditions often go undiagnosed because teenagers can sometimes be sullen and moody naturally. As many as 20 percent of young people in the United States will suffer from some degree of depression before adulthood.

Many parents believe their teenagers go through moody stages and will eventually grow out of their problems. By the time parents or school counselors realize a teen may be struggling with mental health issues, it may be too late—the teen may have already committed suicide.

Girls More Than Boys

Based in Washington DC, the American Association of Suicidology studies trends in suicide. According to the organization, 8.5 percent of students in grades 9 through 12 make at least one suicide attempt at least once a year. Among adults, men attempt suicide more than women, but among adolescents, girls make twice as many attempts as boys. The association has reported that 11.5 percent of teenage girls and 5.4 percent of teenage boys engage in suicidal behaviors. The statistics may be due to the larger number of girls who suffer from borderline personality disorder in adolescence.

Mental health professionals find that teenagers often overreact to what may otherwise be minor problems. For example, their angst over bringing home poor grades may overwhelm them. Part of the fault for that may rest with their parents: today, many young people rarely experience failure. Whether in academics, sports, or hobbies, parents go to great lengths to make sure their children succeed so they can win admissions to top colleges. Many parents spare no expense to provide their children with extra coaching, tutoring, or sessions at summer camps where they

Suicide and Homosexual Teens

Homosexual teens are often isolated from others, confused, shunned, and bullied. All of these factors contribute to a suicide rate that is two to three times higher than that of all other teens. Moreover, a large proportion of homosexual teens attempt suicide. National studies have found that 30 percent of homosexual youths are likely to attempt to kill themselves.

Many teenagers face academic and social challenges during high school. Homosexual youth also face the fear of being ridiculed and rejected because of their sexual preferences. Homophobia, or an extreme dislike of homosexual people, can cause fellow students to deem homosexual high schoolers unacceptable human beings.

Because of the high suicide rate among homosexual teens, some advocacy groups have committed resources to assist these teens. The Trevor Project, based in West Hollywood, California, is one such group. The project was established by the producers of the short film *Trevor*, which told the story of a 13-year-old homosexual boy who attempts suicide. The Trevor Project has sponsored a suicide hotline that fields some 18,000 calls a year from homosexual teens contemplating suicide.

The pressure to succeed academically can prove overwhelming to some teens.

receive intensive training in sports, academics, or the arts.

As a result, when they inevitably do fall short of expectations, some adolescents find themselves unable to confront the realities of failure. To cope, many of them turn to self-destructive and risky behaviors that may include substance abuse, sex, and suicide.

The pressure to succeed may be particularly acute for children born of Asian Americans. These children are often raised by parents who demand success. A 2007 study performed at California State

University-Fullerton found that suicide is the second leading cause of death among Asian Americans between the ages of 15 and 34. The lead researcher, Asian Studies Professor Eliza Noh, said young Asian Americans, particularly girls, face enormous pressure to succeed. Dung Ngo, a psychologist at Baylor University in Texas, added:

> *The line of communication in Asian culture is one way. It's communicated from the parents downward. If you can't express your anger, it turns to helplessness. It turns inward into depression for girls. For boys, it's more likely to turn outwards into rebellious behavior and behavioral problems like drinking and fighting.*[3]

Pacts, Clusters, and Cyber Suicide

Many times, schools and communities are traumatized by news of teenagers who take their own lives, particularly if their suicides occur in clusters or as a result of a pact. These are occasions when two or more people commit suicide together or within a short time of one another. Such suicide pacts are rare, accounting for less than 1 percent of all suicides. Still, when they occur, they send shock waves through a community.

The growth of the Internet is believed to be a contributor to the increase in the adolescent suicide rate. Many teenagers are Web savvy. If they start forming suicidal intentions, they may turn to the Internet for information on how they can carry out their plans. They will find numerous Web sites explaining methods. Some sites even recommend specific drugs and provide advice on how much to consume to ensure the dosages are fatal.

Moreover, the Internet may also lead adolescents and others to make decisions about going ahead with their plans. In 2004, nine people in Japan took their lives after meeting on social networking sites and comparing their ideas about suicide. According to authorities, the victims formed online pacts to commit suicide. In one case, seven of the victims formed a common suicide pact. In the other case, two of the victims agreed to kill themselves. Suicides carried out with the help of the Internet are known as cyber suicides.

Keeping It Quiet

Jeff Barton and Michael Dombroski did not need to rely on the Internet to form their suicide pact. The two boys from East Haddam, Connecticut, were friends. Both found themselves struggling with similar problems.

Barton, 15, had started failing in school and sports. His grades had gone from As and Bs to Fs. He quit the swimming and golf teams. Barton's mother saw the change in his mood and obtained counseling for her son. Soon, he was diagnosed with depression.

Dombroski, 13, was also failing in school and had recently turned to some self-destructive behaviors. He was known to use drugs, come to class under the influence, and argue with his teachers. His older brother had died in a car accident and now he seemed preoccupied with death. Dombroski and his friends spent a lot of time at a local cemetery.

The two boys made a suicide pact. In the early morning hours of May 1, 2000, the teens took the keys of the Dombroski family's vehicle. After driving around town and calling friends, they slammed the vehicle into a tree, killing themselves.

In the days following the incident, police and school officials investigated the deaths. They came

College Students at Risk

A survey of 16,000 college students by the American College Health Association found that 9.5 percent of them had seriously contemplated taking their own lives and 1.5 percent had taken steps to end their lives. In addition, half of the survey respondents said they felt long periods of sadness. One-third said they felt their situations were hopeless, and 22 percent said they felt so depressed they were unable to function.

Suicide Memorials

Friends of suicide victims often create memorials for them. Many mental health experts believe memorials are a bad idea because they may encourage some teens to commit suicide. Such teens may think memorials will bring the love, attention, and esteem in death they believe they lack in life.

Jodi Brandenberger, a counselor who works with teenagers, said, "A child may think, 'I'll never be the homecoming queen, but at least I can memorialize myself with a tree or be in the yearbook.'. . . And they think they'll somehow be able to hang around and see it for themselves."[5]

to the startling revelation that the two teens had told many of their friends of their plans, and none of them thought to contact authorities. As the East Haddam authorities learned, some young people have a very difficult time telling adults about their problems—even if it means helping to avoid potentially fatal circumstances. "Most kids probably would keep it quiet because they don't want to get their friends in trouble," said East Haddam teenager Sam Custin. "If you tell and nothing does happen, you'll face consequences from your friends. You'll be an outcast."[4]

While many young people may feel that confiding in an adult about their concern for a friend is tattling, being open and honest is more important. Speaking with a teacher, a counselor, a coach, or a parent may be difficult, but it will not be as challenging as dealing with the loss of a friend.

German teens mourn the loss of three friends who jumped from a bridge near Reichenbach, Germany, in August 2001.

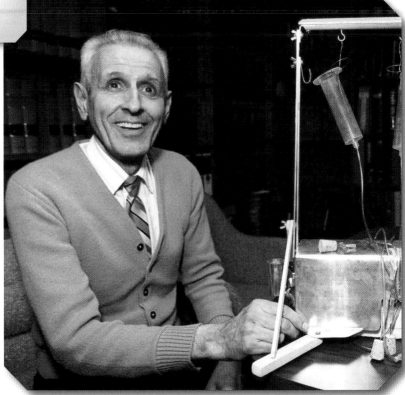

Jack Kevorkian poses with his suicide machine in February 1991.

THE RIGHT TO DIE

ick Farris watched his father and brother die from cancer of the pancreas. Before their deaths, both men suffered for many months. Moreover, their ordeals took a terrible toll on their loved ones. When Farris was also diagnosed with pancreatic cancer, he resolved that his case would be far less painful for everyone.

Farris, a 76-year-old retired photographer, chose the date of his death. As a resident of Oregon, he was able to obtain a doctor's prescription for a lethal dose of barbiturates. Farris said good-bye to his wife and three stepdaughters. Then, he drank the drug. He was dead within five minutes. "[H]e knew what was coming and he didn't want to go through that," said his wife, Gloria. "I found it hard, and I felt left behind—one minute you are talking to your husband . . . the next, he has gone. But it was very much what he wanted."[1]

THE GOOD DEATH

For centuries, society has wrestled with the concept of euthanasia—the act of a terminally ill person to end his or her own life. The word *euthanasia* literally means "good death." However, not everyone has

Debilitated by Disease

Hans Knottenbelt suffered from amyotrophic lateral sclerosis (ALS). Also known as Lou Gehrig's disease, ALS is a debilitating disease that robs patients of their motor control. Many patients die of suffocation. Knottenbelt lived in the Netherlands. After suffering for several years, he elected suicide under the country's euthanasia law. Daughter Karen Knottenbelt said, "My dad woke up in the evenings. . . . scared . . . of the way he would die. . . . The worst thing was that you could see someone you love so dearly . . . with fear in their eyes because . . . they can't get the oxygen that you need in your body. That hurts so much."[2]

always agreed that euthanasia is a good death. Plato was a Greek philosopher who lived during the fourth century BCE. He advocated euthanasia for ill people who wanted to die. Another influential Greek, Hippocrates—"the father of medicine"—found it an unacceptable alternative.

During medieval times, Christians believed their sickness and pain was the will of God. To escape their suffering through suicide meant defying God. By the sixteenth century, influential doctors and philosophers spoke in favor of euthanasia. They argued that people

The Hippocratic Oath

It is unknown whether Hippocrates, the Greek physician who lived during the fourth century BCE, actually wrote the Hippocratic oath. The oath is based on the principles he espoused as one of history's first physicians. Essentially, the oath provides a set of ethical guidelines for doctors, asking them to swear to use their knowledge and abilities for healing.

The classical text of the oath prohibits doctor-assisted suicide. It states, "I will neither give a deadly drug to anybody who asked for it, nor will I make a suggestion to this effect."[3] Today, most medical schools require graduating physicians to recite some version of the oath, but many have altered it to permit euthanasia. A study published in the *Journal of Clinical Ethics* found that only 14 percent of some 150 U.S. and Canadian medical schools include language in their oaths prohibiting doctor-assisted suicide.

The oaths also cover other issues. These include promises to protect patient privacy, respect their teachers, and pass on their skills to others. Every physician is free to interpret the oath as he or she desires. Many doctors may have strong moral feelings against euthanasia, even though their oaths may permit it.

with terminal diseases and no hope for recovery should not be made to suffer through intense pain.

In 1536, French physician Ambroise Paré advocated euthanasia after accompanying a conquering army into a city. Paré came across three wounded soldiers. A fourth soldier asked Paré whether the suffering men had any chance of recovering. When Paré said no, the soldier drew his knife and slit their throats. Paré saw how the men's suffering had been ended quickly in an act of compassion and thereafter advocated euthanasia for the terminally ill.

Society has been slow to accept the concept of euthanasia, particularly following World War II. During the war, the Nazis executed tens of thousands of sick, infirm, and elderly people, believing they were a burden. People are afraid of following such an example. They also fear that the practice will devalue society's view of life. Euthanasia objectors argue that all life is sacred, even life compromised by disease or disability.

Dr. Death

In 1990, Michigan doctor Jack Kevorkian started assisting terminally ill patients who wanted to take their own lives. Kevorkian had developed a device that employed an intravenous tube to inject a fatal dose of life-ending drugs into the patient's bloodstream. Although Kevorkian hooked the patients to the machine, they themselves flipped the switch to start the fatal flow into their veins. Between 1990 and 1998, Kevorkian is believed to have assisted in the suicides of 130 people. Reporters soon learned of Kevorkian's activities and labeled him "Dr. Death."

In 1998, Kevorkian permitted the news show *60 Minutes* to broadcast a video of him assisting in the death of a patient. In this case, Kevorkian actually injected the patient with the drugs because the patient was too debilitated to manipulate the switch on Kevorkian's machine. There was no question that the patient had given his consent to Kevorkian, but when prosecutors saw the video, they charged Kevorkian with murder. He was convicted and sentenced to 10 to 25 years in prison but was released on good behavior after serving eight years.

DEATH WITH DIGNITY

Even as debate over Kevorkian's activities raged in courtrooms and the media, some government

Jack Kevorkian and his attorney hold a $20,000 award granted to Kevorkian in 1995 by a millionaire who champions individual freedoms.

officials and voters gave serious weight to the issue of doctor-assisted suicide. In 1994, voters in Oregon adopted a referendum giving permission to doctors to provide terminally ill patients with drugs that would end their lives.

Enactment of Oregon's Death with Dignity Act was delayed by legal challenges until January 17,

**Death with Dignity
Patients in Oregon**

By the end of 2008, 401
terminally ill patients in
Oregon chose to end their
lives under the state's
Death with Dignity law.
Of those patients, 328 suffered from cancer. Other
illnesses afflicting the
patients included heart
disease, AIDS, and amyo-
trophic lateral sclerosis.

2006, when the U.S. Supreme Court
ruled that states have the power to
regulate doctor-assisted suicide.
In 2008, voters in Washington
approved a similar referendum. In
early 2009, the state's Death with
Dignity law took effect. In Montana,
doctors are permitted to assist in
suicides as a result of a court ruling
in a lawsuit. By early 2009, that case
was on appeal, meaning doctor-
assisted suicide in that state could be
overturned by a Montana Supreme
Court ruling.

However, this does not mean
doctor-assisted suicide is confined
to only those states that have made
the practice legal. A recent study by
the *New England Journal of Medicine* found
that 16 percent of doctors admitted
to giving lethal doses of drugs to
terminally ill patients who requested
them. "Aid in dying happens in every
state," says Patty Berg, a member
of the California Assembly who

sponsored a right-to-die bill in her state. "We need to bring it out of the closet, impose legal safeguards and careful oversight."[4]

A majority of people in the United States appear to favor doctor-assisted suicide. A poll by the Gallup Organization in 2007 found that 56 percent of U.S. residents believe it is acceptable for doctors to assist in the suicides of terminally ill patients; 38 percent are opposed.

Beyond the United States, three European nations have also accepted euthanasia. The Netherlands, Switzerland, and Belgium have adopted laws permitting doctor-assisted suicide. While doctor-assisted suicide is legal in some U.S. states and a few other countries, doctor reluctance could ultimately thwart some terminally ill patients from receiving aid in their suicides. Many physicians take their Hippocratic oaths literally and believe it is the

"Some doctors do intentionally end their patients' lives; others prescribe medications along with a wink and a nod, and the words, 'If you take more than x number of these capsules, you'll die.' Right-to-die advocates argue that, since doctors are intentionally ending their patients' lives now, it would be far better to legalize the practices so that there could be safeguards."[5]
—Rita L. Marker,
executive director,
International Task Force
on Euthanasia and
Assisted Suicide

purpose of medicine to cure, not to hasten death.

Soon after Washington's Death with Dignity law went into effect, physician Stu Farber of the University of Washington Medical Center said he would probably assist in suicides. However, he would do so only in the most heart-wrenching cases. "I am not here to tell people how they should either live their life or the end of their life," he said. "There's possibly a story out there, in the future, that's so compelling that maybe I would write a prescription."[6]

Decriminalizing Euthanasia

Many countries have not legalized assisted suicide. However, Finland, Uruguay, and Estonia have decriminalized it. They do not prosecute doctors or others who provide lethal doses of drugs to patients. In other countries, judges are known to be lenient with family members who assist in the suicides of terminally ill relatives. In Australia, a judge convicted a man of aiding the suicide of his wife but suspended his sentence, giving him no jail time for the act. France and Luxembourg do not regard assisting suicide a crime—prosecutions for the offense are rare and penalties are lenient.

Dr. Robert Thompson says he has treated patients who would have benefited from Washington's Death with Dignity law.

A Japanese kamikaze plane dives at a U.S. warship somewhere in the Pacific Ocean in June 1945.

WHEN SUICIDE
IS A WEAPON

he history books contain many stories about warriors and entire armies who, when faced with defeat, sacrificed their lives to kill as many of their enemies as possible. They embarked on these missions knowing they would surely die, but they

chose a suicidal course rather than
surrender.

In 1831, for example, a Dutch
naval commander named Jan van
Speijk chose to blow up his own
boat rather than surrender to his
enemy. When ordered by the Belgian
invaders to take down the Dutch
flag, Van Speijk responded, "I would
rather blow myself up."[1] He then
touched off a keg of dynamite, killing
himself, 28 members of his crew,
and dozens of Belgians. As for
Van Speijk, he is regarded as a
national hero in the Netherlands.

> **The Murder
> of Alexander II**
>
> Russian Tsar Alexander
> II was assassinated in
> 1881. The tsar was killed
> by a suicide bomber,
> Ignacy Hryniewiecki. He
> detonated the device as
> Alexander II's carriage
> rode by on a street in St.
> Petersburg, Russia.

THE DIVINE WIND

Much more devastating attacks were committed
during the closing months of World War II. Japanese
leaders realized they could not stall the approaching
Allied naval invasion of their country using
conventional air defense tactics. To drop bombs on
enemy ships from a safe distance, pilots had to fly
too high to guarantee accuracy. However, swooping
low risked destruction by antiaircraft fire. So, the

Japanese adopted the strategy of using kamikaze pilots to attack Allied warships.

The noses of the kamikaze planes were outfitted with bombs. Pilots assigned to the missions were instructed to dive their planes into the ships, guaranteeing direct hits. Pilots would not return from kamikaze missions. The word *kamikaze* is Japanese for "divine wind." Kamikaze pilots were regarded as national heroes because they were considered the last, best hope for the Japanese empire to survive.

Futile Strategy

Although the use of kamikazes during World War II resulted in the destruction or damage of hundreds of U.S. vessels, the strategy turned out to be a futile one. Most of the attacks were staged during the three-month Battle of Okinawa that was fought in spring 1945. The Japanese lost the battle and the war.

Some 1,000 pilots flew kamikaze missions during the closing months of the war. Their efforts resulted in the sinking of 36 U.S. warships and severe damage to another 368 craft. Approximately 5,000 U.S. sailors died in the attacks.

The Holy Martyrs

Today, the use of suicide as a weapon has become a common story on the evening news. Middle Eastern countries such as Iran, Jordan, Kuwait, and Syria rank at the bottom of the World Health Organization's 2008 list of suicide rates. But the Middle East has become known worldwide for suicide. Suicide bombings in Iraq, Afghanistan, and other volatile places in the Middle East have cost thousands of lives and hindered efforts to pursue peace. Many U.S. citizens first learned of the tactic in 1983 when a suicide bomber rammed a truck full of explosives into a U.S. Marines barracks in Beirut, Lebanon. More than 200 marines were killed.

Suicide bombers do not fit the profile of suicidal patients: they are not

Self-immolation in South Vietnam

On June 11, 1963, the world suddenly recognized the volatile conditions in South Vietnam when a Buddhist monk set himself on fire. Quang Duc sat down in the middle of a Saigon street and, with the help of other monks, doused himself with gasoline. He then lit a match. The flames engulfed his body, killing him within seconds. The next day, hundreds of newspapers worldwide displayed a grisly photograph of the monk's suicide on their front pages.

The monk's act of self-immolation was intended as a political statement—he wanted to illustrate the mistreatment of Buddhists by South Vietnam's oppressive regime. Later, other Buddhist monks also set themselves on fire. In South Vietnam, the regime of President Ngo Dinh Diem insisted that the monks were prompted into their suicidal acts by communist agents from North Vietnam bent on bringing down the Diem government. The attitude of South Vietnamese leaders toward the monks was most famously articulated by Madame Ngo Dinh Nhu, the president's sister-in-law, who said, "Let them burn, and we shall clap our hands."[2]

believed to suffer from mental disorders usually associated with those who commit suicide. Scott Atran is an adjunct professor at the University of Michigan's Department of Psychology. He also conducts research at the university's Research Center for Group Dynamics. He says of suicide bombers:

> *There's this knee-jerk reaction that people who do this have to be maniacs or cowards, uneducated or miserable or in despair, and none of this seems to be true at all. These people are fairly well educated, mostly from middle class and not acting at all in despair.*[3]

In fact, the Islamic terrorist group Hamas and other terrorist groups typically look for educated young men to serve in the ranks of the *Shaheed*, an Arabic term that means "holy martyrs." However, more and more women and children are being enlisted as suicide bombers. Because these individuals often are not regarded as threatening, security guards may overlook them as they slip into crowded places.

Once they are accepted into the Shaheed, potential bombers undergo weeks or months of indoctrination and training. Atran explains, "These organizations often use religion and religious rites

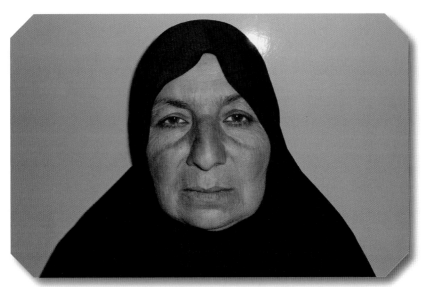

Samira Ahmed Jassim was arrested in 2009. She is suspected of recruiting suicide bombers and has admitted to masterminding 28 bombings.

to create a sort of ritual communion, or bonding, among would-be bombers."[4] They are spurred into the act by terrorists who convince them it is their duty to kill the enemies of Islam. Potential bombers also are told they will be rewarded for their martyrdom in heaven by God, or *Allah* in Arabic. A leader of Hamas told the *New Yorker* magazine:

> *We focus his attention on Paradise, on being in the presence of Allah, on meeting the Prophet Muhammad, on interceding for his loved ones so that they, too, can be saved from the agonies of Hell. . . .* [5]

The case of Ismail al-Masawabi offers a typical example of a promising young man drafted by terrorists as a combatant in jihad, an Arabic term for holy struggle. Al-Masawabi lived in poverty in the Palestinian Territory of Gaza but seemed to have a bright future—he was soon to graduate from a university. Just weeks before graduation, al-Masawabi strapped bombs to his body, walked into a crowded street, and detonated the explosives. He killed himself and two Israeli soldiers. In response, al-Masawabi's mother said:

> *I was very happy when I heard. To be a martyr, that's something. Very few people can do it. I prayed to thank God. In the Koran [Islam's holy book] it's said that a martyr does not die. I know my son is close to me. It is our belief.*[6]

A memorable example of suicide bombing occurred on

"Striving in the Cause of Allah"

Islamic terrorist Fathi Shiqaqi wrote that the goal of all suicide bombers is the *jihad fi sabeel Allah*, "striving in the cause of Allah." Shiqaqi said, "We cannot achieve the goal of these operations if our [holy warrior] is not able to create an explosion within seconds and is unable to prevent the enemy from blocking the operation. All these results can be achieved through the explosion, which forces the [holy warrior] not to waver, not to escape; to execute a successful operation for religion and jihad; and to destroy the morale of the enemy and plant terror into the people."[7]

September 11, 2001, when suicide bombers recruited by the al-Qaeda terrorist network hijacked four U.S. airliners. The men flew planes into both buildings of the World Trade Center in New York City and one into the Pentagon in Washington DC. The fourth plane crashed into a field in rural Pennsylvania. The terrorists' actions took the lives of some 3,000 victims. Israel W. Charny, a psychology professor at Hebrew University in Israel, stated:

> *The nature of the suicide-killing act is so dramatic that it has galvanized worldwide attention, concern, and a desire to understand how the suicide bombers can possibly commit their acts.*

> *The actions of the suicide bombers so contradict the survival instinct that it is hard to understand how they can do it. Suicide bombing is a strange act to the rational mind. It is an act that dramatically combines in one fell blast profound violations of two widely accepted moral standards—the prohibition against killing oneself, and the Thou Shalt Not Kill prohibition against taking other people's lives.*[8]

ISLAM IS A PEACEFUL RELIGION

Many times, the families of bombers are promised financial rewards. After al-Masawabi's

No Paradise for Suicide Bombers

Many Islamic scholars maintain that suicide bombing does not fit the tenets of Islam. Contrary to what they are told by the leaders of terrorist groups, suicide bombers will not be rewarded after death for their deeds. Scholars point to this statement by the Prophet Muhammad: "He who commits suicide by throttling shall keep on throttling himself in the Hell-fire and he who commits suicide by stabbing himself shall keep on stabbing himself in the Hell-fire."[10]

death, Hamas provided his family with financial aid. This enabled them to move out of a refugee camp and into a comfortable Gaza City apartment.

Nevertheless, many Islamic leaders condemn suicide bombing. They argue that Muhammad, who first laid out the tenets of Islam some 1,500 years ago, denounced suicide as an unholy act. They maintain that Islam is a peaceful religion and Muhammad intended jihad to mean an inner struggle in which Muslims strive to resist sin. "It is true that suicide is strictly forbidden, because it is an affront to God," says Adil Salahi, an Islamic historian. "It is like a person saying to God, 'You have given me life and I am taking it away.'"[9]

On September 11, 2001, suicide bombers flew two jet airliners into the
World Trade Center towers in New York City.

Suicide affects many more people than solely the individuals who die.

THE PEOPLE
LEFT BEHIND

eople who commit suicide cut short lives full of promise. They also leave behind friends and family members who must face the heartache and suffering caused by their deaths. Sometimes, those survivors never recover from the anguish caused by the sudden and unexplainable loss of people who were so close to them. George Howe Colt, author of *The Enigma of Suicide*, wrote:

> The suffering of survivors is acute after any death, but the grief inflicted by suicide may be the hardest of all to bear. In addition to shock, denial, anger, and sorrow, the suicide survivor often faces an added burden of guilt and shame.[1]

According to the suicidology.org Web site, a suicide prevention and support group, each suicide intimately affects the lives of six people. Therefore, if 32,000 people take their lives each year, 192,000 people are left behind to suffer through the loss of their loved ones. Survivors may constantly ask themselves what they could have done to prevent their family members or friends from killing themselves.

Long Periods of Anguish

Some survivors of suicide victims face long periods of anguish. Canadian teenager Adam Potash of Winnipeg was a straight-A student and an athlete. He also suffered from depression. At the age of 19, Adam Potash took his own life.

The Potash family had been close. Adam's parents and two brothers were devastated by his death. After her son's suicide, Marlene Potash fell into a state of depression. She found it difficult to get out of bed in the morning and attempted to take her own life. Eventually, Marlene and other members of the family sought counseling to learn to cope.

Since his death, Adam's two brothers have gone on to college. Meanwhile, Adam's father has coped by continuing to do many of the activities he formerly shared with Adam— listening to music,

The Financial Cost of Suicide

In addition to the emotional cost of suicide, there is a monetary cost. Economists have looked into the cost of suicide in terms of dollars and cents. They have concluded that suicides and attempted suicides cost the U.S. economy some $33 billion a year.

According to statistics cited in a 2007 study by the University of Georgia, those costs include more than $32 billion in wages lost by people who kill themselves or become incapacitated by the injuries they sustain in their attempts. The figure also includes the loss in productivity suffered by companies whose employees are left behind as survivors. Those employees often take leaves of absence to deal with their grief and may also suffer depression themselves. Also, the cost of suicide and attempted suicide includes $1 billion in medical expenses for people who survive suicide attempts and surviving family members who may require mental health services.

On an individual basis, the study found that each nonfatal suicide attempt results in $7,234 in medical costs and $9,726 in lost productivity. Each fatal suicide attempt results in $2,596 in medical costs and $1 million in the cost of lost productivity.

working out at the gym, and playing hockey. Still, years after his son's suicide, Jack Potash has been unable to concentrate on his job. In response to her son's death, Marlene established the group SPEAK, which stands for Suicide Prevention Education Awareness Knowledge. But this was not enough to help her cope with the loss of Adam. Marlene Potash killed herself in 2006.

Emotional and Physical Wounds

In addition to family and friends, there are others who must face the harsh consequences of suicide—those who attempt to take their own lives and fail. According to the suicide.org Web site, approximately 5 million people in the United States have attempted suicide at some point in their lives.

Many of the people who survive their suicide attempts each year are left with emotional and physical wounds. They may suffer from gunshot wounds that leave them with traumatic brain injuries that affect their abilities to function, concentrate, and support themselves. Many who try to take their own lives by jumping from high places succeed only in sustaining serious injuries to their legs or backs. Some are incapacitated for life.

Daniel Harris grew up near Oklahoma City, Oklahoma. He had a difficult childhood. Harris's parents divorced. He dropped out of high school and spent a lot of time going to parties. In his twenties, though, Harris turned his life around. He earned his general equivalency diploma and then enrolled in college in Nebraska. Soon, Harris and his girlfriend made plans to marry.

But Harris's mother died and his relationship with his girlfriend grew stormy and, finally, the couple broke up. Harris started drinking heavily. One day, he showed up at his girlfriend's house intoxicated. When she left him alone for a few minutes, Harris tried to hang himself. When the paramedics arrived 20 minutes later, they found Harris unconscious but alive.

When the noose pulled tight around Harris's neck, his brain was denied the blood and oxygen it needed to survive. In response to the trauma, Harris's brain expanded, pressing against his skull and causing internal bleeding. Doctors were able to stabilize his condition. He returned to consciousness,

Spinal Injuries Common

A 1999 British study looked at the number of debilitating spinal injuries suffered by people who attempt to kill themselves by jumping from high places. The study found that in 137 failed suicide attempts, 116 people suffered spinal cord injuries, and most permanently lost the use of their legs.

but the injury severely—perhaps permanently—damaged his brain.

Since leaving the hospital, Harris has exhibited delusional behavior and memory impairment. He does not remember his former girlfriend or the fact that he had been enrolled in college. He has trouble recalling the day of the week. During his stay in a rehabilitation hospital, his father, Shane Harris, took him out to play golf. "In the course of one game of golf, he asked me the same three questions over sixty times," said Shane Harris. "What did I do, why am I here, and where is my mom? He was like a little kid again."[2]

Meanwhile, Shane Harris has served as his son's guardian. He has dealt with the legal issues and government bureaucracy involved in his son's commitment to rehabilitation hospitals. Virtually penniless at the time of his attempted suicide, Daniel Harris's care is financed by the state of Nebraska. According to Shane Harris, keeping up with the paperwork required for Daniel to continue receiving

Conflicted Emotions

After 21 years of marriage, Carla Fine lost her husband, Harry, to suicide. Fine was angry at him for leaving her and for burdening her with grief. Fine said, "Suicide is different from other deaths. We who are left behind cannot direct our anger at the unfairness of a deadly disease or a random accident or a murderous stranger. Instead, we grieve for the very person who has taken our loved one's life. Before we can even begin to accept our loss, we must deal with the reasons for it—and the gradual recognition that we might never know what happened or why."[3]

The Saturday before
Thanksgiving is National
Survivors of Suicide Day.
It was created in 1999
by a resolution in Con-
gress authored by Senate
Majority Leader Harry
Reid, who lost his father to
suicide. On that day, the
American Foundation for
Suicide Prevention works
with local survivors to
organize more than 170
conferences nationwide.
The conferences examine
the causes of suicide and
the challenges faced by
survivors.

care is almost a full-time job. As
for Daniel Harris, even though he
continues to receive round-the-
clock rehabilitation, his mental and
physical abilities are deteriorating.
Two years after his attempted suicide,
Harris's brain trauma case manager,
Michael Paul Mason, described a
meeting with him:

> *Daniel's tone is flat and despondent;
> I ache just to hear him talk. . . . His
> motor coordination has deteriorated
> significantly; he won't be able to hit
> a golf ball, much less walk an entire
> game of golf anymore. The remainder
> of our conversation consists mainly of
> monosyllabic replies from Daniel . . .*

*Daniel regularly asks for permission to call his mother. He
sleeps in all morning long. He turns down meals almost daily.
He isolates as much as possible. The social worker tells me
that while Daniel isn't a behavioral problem, he has lashed
out by yelling at others and hitting them. I don't know that I
would act any more civil if the same thing happened to me.*[4]

It can be difficult to cope with the suicide of a loved one.

CRISIS COUNSELING

THERE IS HOPE
MAKE THE CALL

THE CONSEQUENCES OF
JUMPING FROM THIS
BRIDGE ARE FATAL
AND TRAGIC.

*The Golden Gate Bridge has been a popular suicide site. The city
of San Francisco installed a crisis phone line on the bridge.*

PREVENTING SUICIDES

There are many strategies for preventing
suicides. Suicide hotlines offer short-term
help and are available in many communities. Staffed
by professionals or trained volunteers, they often
provide the suicidal person with support simply by

listening to and speaking with the caller. In most cases, people who call suicide hotlines just need someone who will listen to them and provide them with alternatives.

Rick Baumann has been volunteering at the Suicide Prevention Service in Columbus, Ohio, for 16 years. He started working for the community-based service shortly after his teenage son Gabriel attempted to kill himself. Gabriel survived the attempt—although, years later, he did take his own life.

Baumann has vowed to do what he can to prevent others from committing suicide. Since his son's first attempt, he has logged more than 5,000 hours on the phone helping suicidal people find a way to cope with their problems.

EFFECTIVENESS OF ANTIDEPRESSANTS

If a suicidal person is undergoing psychiatric treatment, chances are he or she is taking antidepressant medication. According to a 2007

Side Effects

Antidepressants provide relief to many people. They also may cause unintended effects. Common side effects include diarrhea, dry mouth, fatigue, and weight gain or loss. Some patients may actually experience an increase in suicidal thoughts and actions, especially those younger than 25. Antidepressant labels include warnings about the possibility of such effects in young people.

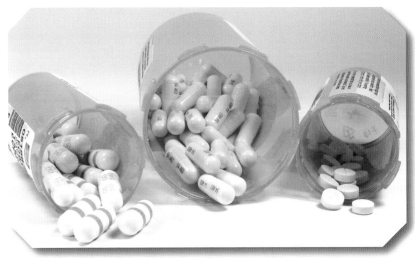

Medications such as fluoxetine, lithium, and cytomel can benefit those who suffer from mental disorders.

study published in the *American Journal of Psychiatry*, antidepressants have proven effective in controlling suicidal ideation. Furthermore, suicide attempts recede over time among patients who take antidepressants. Antidepressants are effective in controlling impulsive behaviors, a prime factor in most suicide attempts.

Many common antidepressants, including Prozac, Paxil, and Zoloft, work by maintaining high levels of the neurotransmitter serotonin in the brain. Neurotransmitters are chemicals that carry messages from brain cell to brain cell,

regulating emotions and other human functions.
Serotonin regulates anger, aggression, mood, body
temperature, sleep, and appetite. It is believed that
depressed people, including those who have suicidal
ideations, suffer from a lack of serotonin. The
American Journal of Psychiatry study cited statistics showing
the rate of suicide among depressed people not
taking antidepressants is three times that of people
who do take the drugs.

MORE THAN DRUG THERAPY

However, many people who take antidepressants
still attempt suicide. Mental health professionals are
convinced that it takes more than drug therapy to
help a patient overcome suicidal intentions.

Many patients, particularly those suffering from
borderline personality disorder, have benefited
from cognitive behavioral therapy. The therapy has
been used for many years to help people overcome
phobias. By participating in cognitive behavioral
therapy, a person who is afraid of heights would take
small steps to conquer his or her fear. For example,
in the first session of therapy, the patient who fears
heights may take an elevator to the second floor of a
skyscraper. In the next session, the patient may ride

to the fourth floor. Session by session, the phobic learns to conquer his or her fear by going a little bit higher until he or she reaches the top floor of the skyscraper.

The therapy works for other patients with mental disorders as well, including those who are borderline and engage in self-destructive behaviors. To begin, psychologists and psychiatrists work with patients to find the root of their problems. Next, they develop strategies to confront these causes. Much as the phobic afraid of heights learns to take small steps to the top of a skyscraper, this patient will improve gradually. He or she will find ways to deal with stresses that are not self-destructive.

University of Washington psychologist Marsha Linehan has pioneered cognitive behavioral therapy for borderline patients. According to her, "You have to get these people not to go to the hospital when they're feeling suicidal and at the same time have them feel they're not being left on the floor, that they

Schizophrenia Study

A 2007 British study found that cognitive behavioral therapy is effective in reducing suicidal ideations among schizophrenia patients. The study followed 90 schizophrenia patients, 44 of whom received the therapy over a nine-month period. According to the study's authors, suicidal ideations in the patients went down by 50 percent over the course of their treatments.

have some skills to manage."[1] Learning how to cope can help patients to better manage their actions and ultimately keep them alive and out of the hospital.

What to Do

People who suspect their loved ones are at risk for suicide can look for many warning signs. This includes changes in sleeping and eating habits and feeling constantly weary. Also, at-risk people tend to have poor memories, an inability to concentrate, and changes in performance. People who are at

Teen Suicide Warning Signs

Young people who are thinking about taking their own lives often send out warning signs. Because of the severe consequences of ignoring the signals, mental health experts urge friends of troubled teens to tell parents, teachers, and school counselors about their suspicions.

The National Alliance on Mental Illness has composed a list of warning signs that may suggest troubled teens are thinking about suicide. The signs include:

- Extreme personality changes
- Loss of interest in activities that used to be enjoyable
- Significant loss or gain in appetite
- Difficulty falling asleep or a desire to sleep all day
- Fatigue or loss of energy
- Feelings of worthlessness or guilt
- Withdrawal from families and friends
- Neglect of personal appearance and hygiene
- Sadness, irritability, and indifference
- Trouble with concentration
- Extreme anxiety or episodes of panic
- Drug and alcohol abuse
- Aggressive, destructive, and defiant behavior
- Poor school performance
- Hallucinations and delusional beliefs

risk for suicide suffer from anxiety and feelings of hopelessness and worthlessness. Some are preoccupied with death. Many at-risk people also have a family history of depression and suicide.

Experts on suicide counsel friends and family members to be assertive—not to assume that the suicidal person will get over his or her feelings. "Sometimes, you even have to take the person to the ER," says Paula Clayton, medical director of the American Foundation for Suicide Prevention. "Calling the [suicide] hotline is one thing to do, but it's better to see that the person is evaluated. Don't leave them alone."[2]

Suicide by Cop

The suicide rate may be higher than originally believed. A 2009 study found that more than one-third of the people shot by police officers may have put themselves intentionally in harm's way. Such cases are known as "suicide by cop."

The study examined 707 police shooting cases from 1998 to 2006. In 36 percent of the cases, the individuals threatened, injured, or even killed others in the belief that they would be shot by police officers arriving at the scene. Approximately half of the police shootings were fatal.

SUICIDAL TENDENCIES

In recent years, the U.S. suicide rate has been climbing slowly. In 1999, approximately 29,000 people in the United States took their own lives. In 2005, the number increased to more than 32,000. As the eleventh leading cause of death in the country, suicide now costs the lives of more U.S. residents than liver disease, kidney disease, and high blood pressure. David Satcher is a former U.S. surgeon general. He said:

> I don't think I should have to convince anyone that suicide is a serious public health problem. . . . In recent years, Americans have been very concerned about the number of homicides being committed across the country, but it surprises most people to learn that for every two homicides that take place in the U.S., there are three suicides committed.[3]

Unlike many deadly diseases, suicidal intentions cannot be cured by medical advances alone. Certainly, antidepressant medications help, but mental health professionals acknowledge that they are not the only answer. People who suffer from depression, bipolar disorder, borderline personality disorder, and other illnesses need support from friends and family members. Those who suffer from a mental disorder need people who can recognize the warning signs and help them find ways to resolve their inner turmoil. Satcher believes most suicides are preventable as long as the people who are closest to those at risk know what they must do to prevent a tragedy.

Garrett Lee Smith Memorial Act

In 2004, Congress began providing funds to help community organizations pay for suicide hotlines. Since then, some $80 million has been appropriated to support suicide hotlines under the Garrett Lee Smith Memorial Act. The law was named for the son of former U.S. Senator Gordon Smith of Oregon. Garrett Lee Smith committed suicide while attending college in Utah in 2003.

Satcher and other public health officials believe much work must be done to reverse the trend in suicide. Satcher has called for governments and communities to step up intervention programs. He wants medical researchers to seek new treatments for mental disorders that may spark suicides. He asks the public to gain a better understanding of suicide—to find sympathy for the victims and their families and not to stigmatize survivors. The negative response to victims and survivors isolates them and adds to their sense of guilt and shame. If public health officials succeed, they know many lives in the United States will be saved. Families and friends will be spared the needless loss of their loved ones, and society will benefit from the talents of those who might have died. ⌐

In 1999, Surgeon General David Satcher declared suicide
a serious public health threat for the first time.

TIMELINE

ca. 350 BCE	ca. 50 CE	300s
Greek philosopher Aristotle suggests suicide is an act of cowardice.	Roman orator Seneca says suicide can provide an acceptable means of escape from one's troubles.	Christian scholars denounce suicide, contending it is a sin.

1536	late 1500s	1648
Physician Ambroise Paré advocates euthanasia after watching three mortally wounded soldiers killed to end their suffering.	William Shakespeare writes *Romeo and Juliet*. The play garners widespread empathy for suicide victims.	John Donne publishes his essay *Biathanatos*, which argues suicide should not be regarded as sinful.

500s	1200s	early 1300s
Islamic Prophet Muhammad condemns suicide, finding it unholy.	Japanese samurai warriors who face dishonor are expected to take their own lives through the ritual known as hara-kiri.	Dante begins work on *The Divine Comedy*, placing suicides in the second ring of the Seventh Circle of Hell.

1755	1823	1917
David Hume publishes the essay *Of Suicide*, which argues suicide does not violate morals or the will of God.	The British parliament permits suicide victims to be buried in cemeteries.	Sigmund Freud publishes *Mourning and Melancholia*, which argues that people take their own lives as way to act out their hostilities.

TIMELINE

1938

In *Man Against Himself*, Karl Menninger declares three elements of suicide: the wish to kill, to be killed, and to die.

1978

On November 18, at Jonestown in Guyana, most of the 918 members of the People's Temple commit suicide.

1983

On October 23, a suicide bomber destroys the U.S. Marine barracks in Beirut, Lebanon. More than 200 U.S. servicemen die.

2001

Islamic suicide bomber terrorists attack the United States on September 11.

2004

Nine people in Japan use the Internet to forge suicide pacts.

2006

On January 17, the U.S. Supreme Court upholds Oregon's Death with Dignity Act.

1990	1994	1999
Michigan physician Jack Kevorkian helps the first of 130 terminally ill patients commit suicide.	On November 8, Oregon voters approve the state's Death with Dignity Act.	U.S. Surgeon General David Satcher declares suicide a serious public health threat.

2007	2007–2008	2008
A Gallup Organization poll finds 56 percent of U.S. residents support doctor-assisted suicide.	The economic recession sparks a jump in the number of suicides among middle-age people in the United States.	The U.S. Army reports an increase in suicides among soldiers.

ESSENTIAL FACTS

AT ISSUE

❖ Depression is the primary mental disorder responsible for suicidal ideations. Other mental disorders also contribute to suicide, including bipolar disorder.

❖ Suicides by teenagers and young adults are increasing.

❖ The growth of the Internet is believed to be responsible for the increase in the adolescent suicide rate.

❖ Suicide bombers kill themselves in order to kill others.

❖ Some terminally ill patients want to choose death—or "die with dignity"—rather than suffer a long, painful death.

❖ Survivors of victims of suicide suffer emotionally.

❖ Those who attempt suicide and fail suffer emotionally and, often, physically.

❖ Suicides and attempted suicides cost the U.S. economy an estimated $33 billion a year.

CRITICAL DATES

1300s
Christian scholars denounced suicide.

1536
French physician Ambroise Paré advocated euthanasia.

1938
Karl Menninger declared three elements of suicide.

1983
On October 23, a suicide bomber destroyed the U.S. Marine barracks in Lebanon.

1990
Dr. Jack Kevorkian began helping terminally ill patients commit suicide.

1994
Oregon voters approved the state's Death with Dignity Act.

2001
On September 11, Islamic suicide bombers crashed into the World Trade Center in New York City.

2007–2008
The economic recession sparked a jump in the number of suicides among middle-age people in the United States.

2008
The U.S. Army reported an increase in suicides among soldiers.

QUOTES

"It is unlikely that any one theory will ever explain phenomena as varied and as complicated as human self-destructive behaviors. In general, it is probably accurate to say that suicide always involves an individual's tortured logic in a state of inner-felt, intolerable emotion."—*Edwin S. Shneidman, psychologist*

"The suffering of survivors is acute after any death, but the grief inflicted by suicide may be the hardest of all to bear. In addition to shock, denial, anger, and sorrow, the suicide survivor often faces an added burden of guilt and shame."—*George Howe Colt,* The Enigma of Suicide

ADDITIONAL RESOURCES

SELECT BIBLIOGRAPHY

Charny, Israel W. *Fighting Suicide Bombing: A Worldwide Campaign for Life*. Santa Barbara, CA: Greenwood, 2006.

Colt, George Howe. *The Enigma of Suicide*. New York, NY: Summit, 1991.

Hainer, Michelle. "The Scary Truth About Teen Suicide." *Teen People*. Sept. 2005.

McNamara, Paul, Xana O'Neill, and Carrie Melago. "Russian Supermodel with 'Fairy Tale' Beauty, Age 20, Plummets to Her Death." *New York Daily News*. 29 June 2008. <http://www.nydailynews.com/news/2008/06/28/2008-06-28_russian_supermodel_with_fairytale_beauty.html>.

Megan, Kathleen. "When a Teen Is in Trouble: Code of Silence." *Hartford Courant*. 3 May 2000.

FURTHER READING

Langwith, Jacqueline, ed. *Suicide: Opposing Viewpoints*. Farmington Hills, MI: Greenhaven, 2008.

Salomon, Ron, and Christine Collins. *Suicide*. New York, NY: Chelsea House, 2007.

Taylor, Robert. *The Right To Die*. Farmington Hills, MI: Lucent, 2009.

WEB LINKS

To learn more about suicide, visit ABDO Publishing Company online at **www.abdopublishing.com**. Web sites about suicide are featured on our Book Links page. These links are routinely monitored and updated to provide the most current information available.

For More Information

For more information on this subject, contact or visit the following organizations.

American Association of Suicidology
5221 Wisconsin Avenue NW, Washington, DC 20015
202-237-2280
www.suicidology.org
The association supports research into the causes of suicide and helps train mental health professionals specializing in treating suicidal patients and professionals who work in crisis intervention programs. The organization's Web site offers a variety of statistics and reports on suicide, depression, and how survivors of suicide victims confront their grief.

American Foundation for Suicide Prevention
120 Wall Street, Floor 22, New York, NY 10005
888-333-AFSP (2377)
www.afsp.org
The foundation funds scientific research and supports public education programs to help people recognize the warning signs of suicide.

National Institute of Mental Health
6001 Executive Boulevard, Room 8184, MSC 9663
Bethesda, MD 20892-9663
866-615-6464
www.nimh.nih.gov
The National Institute of Mental Health is the federal government's chief funder of research into mental disorders, including those that prompt patients into suicidal acts.

National Suicide Prevention Lifeline
800-273-8255
www.suicidepreventionlifeline.com
This 24-hour, toll-free hotline is available to anyone in a suicidal crisis.

GLOSSARY

antidepressants
Class of prescription drugs that enhance the flow of the neurotransmitter serotonin, which controls mood.

bipolar disorder
A mental disorder in which a person experiences extremes of emotion, switching between phases of depression and mania.

borderline personality disorder
A mental disorder characterized by impulsiveness, mood swings, and self-destructive behaviors.

cybersuicide
Use of the Internet to form suicide pacts and to find methods to commit suicide.

depression
A mental disorder in which patients often experience feelings of sadness, hopelessness, and inadequacy.

euthanasia
Drawn from Greek words that mean "good death," it is the act of killing or permitting death to end physical suffering.

gallows
A frame of wood with a crossbeam on two uprights that is used for hanging people.

hara-kiri
Suicide ritual practiced by thirteenth-century samurai warriors in Japan who were obliged to kill themselves when faced with dishonor.

Hippocratic oath
Promise taken by graduating medical students to use their powers for healing only, although many medical schools have eliminated language from the oaths prohibiting euthanasia.

Islamic fundamentalist
> A Muslim who adheres to a literal translation of Islamic law and often believes that Islam should be spread through martyrdom, which includes killing nonbelievers through suicide attacks.

martyrdom
> Dying for a cause, particularly for one's religion.

mood disorder
> A psychological illness, such as depression, in which the sufferer struggles with emotions.

paranoia
> A mental disorder in which a person feels threatened by others and has fears and suspicions.

schizophrenia
> A mental disorder characterized by an abnormal perception of reality, including delusional beliefs and hallucinations.

serotonin
> Chemical in the brain that regulates anger, aggression, mood, body temperature, sleep, and appetite.

suicidal ideations
> Thoughts of harming or killing oneself.

suicide
> The act of purposely killing oneself.

suicide attempt
> The failed act of purposely killing oneself.

SOURCE NOTES

Chapter 1. Death of the Russian Rapunzel
1. Paul McNamara, Xana O'Neill, and Carrie Melago. "Russian Supermodel with 'Fairy Tale' Beauty, Age 20, Plummets to Her Death." *New York Daily News*. 29 June 2008. 23 Mar. 2009 <http://www.nydailynews.com/news/2008/06/28/2008-06-28_russian_supermodel_with_fairytale_beauty.html>.
2. Ibid.
3. Cara Buckley. "Young Model's Death Reveals a Life of Isolation." *New York Times*. 5 July 2008: B1.
4. Centers for Disease Control and Prevention. "Suicide Prevention: Definitions." *CDC.org*. 20 Aug. 2008. 23 Mar. 2009 <http://www.cdc.gov/ViolencePrevention/suicide/definitions.html>.
5. Kay Redfield Jamison. *Night Falls Fast: Understanding Suicide*. New York: Knopf, 1999. 26.
6. Veronika Bellenkaya and Corky Siemaszko. "Camera Loved 'Russian Rapunzel' From First Shoot, Photographer Says." *New York Daily News*. 1 July 2008. 23 Mar. 2009 <http://www.nydailynews.com/news/2008/06/30/2008-06-30_camera_loved_russian_rapunzel_from_first.html>.
7. "Excerpts From Model Ruslana Korshunova's Blog." *New York Daily News*. 30 June 2008. 23 Mar. 2009 <http://www.nydailynews.com/news/2008/06/29/2008-06-29_excerpts_from_model_ruslana_korshunovas_.html>.
8. Kay Redfield Jamison. *Night Falls Fast: Understanding Suicide*. New York: Knopf, 1999. 74.

Chapter 2. A History of Suicide
1. Will Durant. *The Story of Civilization III: Caesar and Christ*. New York: Simon and Schuster, 1944. 306.
2. J. A. K. Thompson, trans. *The Ethics of Aristotle*. Middlesex, Eng.: Penguin, 1973. 97.
3. Thomas Stephen Szasz. *Fatal Freedom: The Ethics and Politics of Suicide*. Westport, CT: Praeger, 1999. 14.
4. "Freud and Death." *Time*. 17 July 1972. 23 Mar. 2009 <http://www.time.com/time/magazine/article/0,9171,877882,00.html>.
5. Antoon A. Leenaars, ed. *Lives and Deaths: Selections from the Writings of Edwin S. Shneidman*. Philadelphia: Taylor & Francis, 1999. 177.

Chapter 3. Risk Factors

1. WHO. "Suicide rates per 100,000 by country, year and sex (Table)." *WHO.int*. 2009. 25 June 2009 <http://www.who.int/mental_health/prevention/suicide_rates/en/>.
2. "Surgeon General Lays Out Suicide Prevention Plan." *CNN*. 3 May 2001. 23 Mar. 2009 <http://archives.cnn.com/2001/HEALTH/05/02/suicide.prevention/index.html>.
3. "Why Women Are Less Likely Than Men to Commit Suicide." *Science Daily*. 12 Nov. 1998. 23 Mar. 2009 <http://www.sciencedaily.com/releases/1998/11/981112075159.htm>.
4. Ibid.
5. Luis Martinez. "Army Suicides Rise Sharply." *ABC News*. 5 Feb. 2009. 23 Mar. 2009 <http://abcnews.go.com/Politics/US/story?id=6815050&page=1>.
6. Theresa Tamkins. "Study: U.S. Suicides Rising; Risk High in Middle Age." *CNN*. 21 Oct. 2008. 23 Mar. 2009 <http://www.cnn.com/2008/HEALTH/10/21/Healthmag.suicide.increase>.
7. George Howe Colt. *The Enigma of Suicide*. New York: Summit, 1991. 409.

Chapter 4. Mental Disorders and Suicide

1. National Institute of Mental Health. "Men and Depression." *NIMH Web site*. 3 Apr. 2008. 23 Mar. 2009 <http://www.nimh.nih.gov/health/publications/men-and-depression/complete-index.shtml>.
2. Kay Redfield Jamison. *Night Falls Fast: Understanding Suicide*. New York: Knopf, 1999. 103–104.
3. Christopher Sandford. *Kurt Cobain*. New York: Carroll & Graf, 1996. 10.
4. Patrick Perry. "Personality Disorders: Coping with the Borderline." *Saturday Evening Post*. July-August 1997: 44.
5. Jeffrey Kluger. "The Cruelest Cut." *Time*. 16 May 2005: 48. <http://www.time.com/time/magazine/article/0,9171,1059046,00.html>.
6. A. E. Hotchner. *Papa Hemingway*. New York: Random House, 1966. 274.

Chapter 5. The Youngest Victims
1. George Howe Colt. *The Enigma of Suicide*. New York: Summit, 1991. 38.
2. Michelle Hainer. "The Scary Truth About Teen Suicide." *Teen People*. Sept. 2005: 162.
3. Elizabeth Cohen. "Push to Achieve Tied to Suicide in Asian-American Women." *CNN.com*. 16 May 2007. 8 Apr. 2009 <http://www.cnn.com/2007/HEALTH/05/16/asian.suicides/index.html>.
4. Kathleen Megan. "When A Teen Is in Trouble: Code of Silence." *Hartford Courant*. 3 May 2000: A1.
5. Tom Gorman. "Dealing with Grief—Some Experts Say Establishing Memorials for Young Suicide Victims Is Healthy, but Others Fear It Prompts Imitations." *Los Angeles Times*. 26 Feb. 1995. 20 July 2009 <http://articles.latimes.com/1995-02-26/news/mn-36359_1_teen-suicide-victims>.

Chapter 6. The Right to Die
1. Jo Revill. "I said, 'I'll See You in the Morning.' He said, 'Ok...' Then He Went to Sleep." *London Observer*. 5 Dec. 2004. 23 Mar. 2009 <http://www.guardian.co.uk/society/2004/dec/05/health.medicineandhealth>.
2. Michael Petrou. "A Time to Die." *Maclean's*. 5 Sept. 2005: 22.
3. "The Hippocratic Oath: Classical Version." *Doctor's Diaries*. 2009. *WGBH Educational Foundation*. 23 Mar. 2009 <http://www.pbs.org/wgbh/nova/doctors/oath_classical.html>.
4. Margot Roosevelt. "Choosing Their Time." *Time*. 4 Apr. 2005: 31.
5. Rita L. Marker. "Euthanasia and Assisted Suicide Today." *Society*. May-June 2006: 59.
6. Rachel La Corte. "'Death with Dignity' Law in Washington State." *Philadelphia Inquirer*. 2 Mar. 2009: A2.

Chapter 7. When Suicide Is a Weapon
1. "Suicide Bombing: The First Was a Christian." *Sky News*. 27 July 2005. 8 Apr. 2009 <http://news.sky.com/skynews/Home/Sky-News-Archive/Article/20080641190443>.
2. Stanley Karnow. *Vietnam: A History*. New York: Penguin, 1997. 297.
3. "Profile: Look at the Mind of a Suicide Bomber." *Morning Edition*. 7 Mar. 2003. National Public Radio. 7 May 2009 <http://www.npr.org/programs/morning/transcripts/2003/mar/030307.joyce.html>.

4. Ibid.

5. Nasra Hassan. "An Arsenal of Believers." *New Yorker*. 19 Nov. 2001. 23 Mar. 2009 <http://www.newyorker.com/archive/2001/11/19/011119fa_FACT1>.

6. Joseph Lelyveld. "All Suicide Bombers Are Not Alike." *New York Times Sunday Magazine*. 28 Oct. 2001: 50.

7. Nasra Hassan. "An Arsenal of Believers." *New Yorker*. 19 Nov. 2001. 23 Mar. 2009 <http://www.newyorker.com/archive/2001/11/19/011119fa_FACT1>.

8. Israel W. Charny. *Fighting Suicide Bombing: A Worldwide Campaign for Life*. Santa Barbara, CA: Greenwood, 2006. 2.

9. Adil Salahi. "Committing Suicide Is Strictly Forbidden in Islam." *Al Jazeerah*. 22 June 2004. 23 Mar. 2009 <http://www.aljazeerah.info/Islam/Islamic%20subjects/2004%20subjects/June/Committing%20Suicide%20Is%20Strictly%20Forbidden%20in%20Islam,%20Adil%20Salahi.htm>.

10. Muhammad Taqi-ud-Din Al-Hilali and Muhammad Muhsin Khan. *Interpretation of the Noble Qur'an in the English Language*. Riyadh, Saud.: Darussalam, 1999. 121.

Chapter 8. The People Left Behind

1. George Howe Colt. *The Enigma of Suicide*. New York: Summit, 1991. 409.

2. Michael Paul Mason. *Head Cases: Stories of Brain Injury and Its Aftermath*. New York: Farrar, Straus and Giroux, 2008. 259.

3. Carla Fine. *No Time to Say Goodbye: Surviving the Suicide of a Loved One*. New York: Main Street, 1999. 13.

4. Michael Paul Mason. *Head Cases: Stories of Brain Injury and Its Aftermath*. New York: Farrar, Straus and Giroux, 2008. 271.

Chapter 9. Preventing Suicides

1. Benedict Carey. "So Far, Holding Up Under Scrutiny." *New York Times*. 13 July 2004: F6.

2. Leah Chernikoff. "When Someone's At Risk, There Are Ways You Can Help." *New York Daily News*. 1 July 2008: 27.

3. David Satcher. "Remarks at the Release of the Surgeon General's Call to Action to Prevent Suicide." *Office of the Surgeon General*. 28 July 1999. 23 Mar. 2009 <http://www.surgeongeneral.gov/library/calltoaction/remarks.htm>.

INDEX

ABOUT THE AUTHOR

Hal Marcovitz is a former newspaper reporter who has written more than 120 books for young readers. In 2005, *Nancy Pelosi*, his biography of House Speaker Nancy Pelosi, was named to *Booklist* magazine's list of recommended feminist books for young readers. As a journalist, he won three Keystone Press Awards, the highest award for newspaper reporting presented by the Pennsylvania Newspaper Association. He lives in Chalfont, Pennsylvania, with his wife and daughter.

PHOTO CREDITS

iStockphoto, cover, 57, 86; WWD/Condé Nast/Corbis, 6; Rhienna Cutler/iStockphoto, 11; Diane Bondareff/AP Images, 15; North Wind Picture Archives, 16, 19, 96 (top), 96 (bottom); AP Images, 25, 68; Jose Gil/iStockphoto, 26; Red Line Editorial, 28; Gord Horne/iStockphoto, 31; Zoran Ivanovic/iStockphoto, 37, 99 (bottom); iStockphoto, 38; Frank Micelotta/Stringer/ Getty Images, 42; A. E. Hotchner/AP Images, 47; E. J. White/ Shutterstock Images, 48; Willie B. Thomas/iStockphoto, 52; Richard Sheinwald/AP Images, 58, 63, 99 (top); Ted S. Warren/ AP Images, 67; Qassim Abdul-Zahra/AP Images, 73; Carmen Taylor/AP Images, 77, 98; Aldo Murillo/iStockphoto, 78, 97; Sheryl Griffin/iStockphoto, 85; Paige Foster/iStockphoto, 88; Ron Edmonds/AP Images, 95